To the Rees f[amily]

hoping you w[ill come]
to Oz to sample
the cuisine & friends
soon.

love from
Christine, Dick, Beth & Robin
July 2001

A LITTLE FLAVOUR

of

AUSTRALIA

Published by J.D.Publishing
Olaski Pty.Ltd.
ACN 002 856 402
P.O.Box 778 St.Ives N.S.W. 2075
AUSTRALIA.

ISBN   0 - 646 - 36724 - 2
Printed in China by Toppan Printing.
Except where otherwise stated, recipes are for four persons.
Accessories and china by Hospitality Warehouse. Brookvale, Sydney.
Wines by Kingston Estate, Riverland district, South Australia.

CONTENTS

SOUPS & STARTERS

FISH & SHELLFISH

MEAT & POULTRY

VEGETABLES & SALADS

PASTA & RICE

BREAD, CAKES & BISCUITS

DESSERTS

INTRODUCTION

Our culinary heritage is most certainly an eclectic one.
Indigenous Australians' basic cooking methods
were observed by the early European settlers and fused
with their own concepts. These were already changing to make
full use of their new found bounty of fruits, nuts, vegetation,
seafood and game, native to our coastal fringes.
Later, with introduced crops and animals, variations on
traditional British fare developed. Through the following
years,we have become a multicultural society. From the early
Chinese gold prospectors, through to the post war European
immigration program and latterly the full spectrum of Asian
nations, African, Indian, Polynesian, Arabic. In fact there is
almost no province which has not had some bearing on the
nature of our eating habits today.
We have endeavoured here to capture a cross section of them all
without being either old school or nouvelle. Above all we hope
that should you take this book to your homeland overseas,
you will find it adapts easily to your available ingredients and
that you are still able to enjoy

A little flavour of Australia.

soups and starters

corn fritters
with mango mayo

tablespoon Oil - six Corn cobs - one clove Garlic (minced)
teaspoon Turmeric - tablespoon Red Capsicum (chopped finely)
tablespoon Green Capsicum (chopped finely)
four Eggs - 2/3 cup Plain Flour
Salt - Black Pepper - 1/2 cup Mayonnaise - 1/2 cup Sour Cream
1 1/2 dessertspoons Sweet Chilli Sauce - Flesh of One Mango.

Slice the corn off the cobs. Combine in a bowl with minced garlic,
turmeric, capsicum and one dessertspoon of sweet chilli sauce.
In another bowl beat the eggs and add the flour.
Add the two mixtures together and season to taste.
Heat the oil in a shallow pan and drop spoonfulls of mixture,
a few at a time into the pan and fry until crisp both sides.

Process together the mayonnaise, sour cream, mango and half a
dessertspoon of sweet chilli sauce. Serve on top of the fritters.

pizza
with beetroot jam and potato

2 1/2 Tablespoons Olive Oil - 850 gm. tin Beetroot
one teaspoon yellow mustard seed - one teaspoon Ground Cloves
two Onions peeled and chopped - 150 mls Malt Vinegar
1 1/2 cups Brown Sugar - three potatoes
four rashers of lean Bacon - 3/4 Cup shredded Mozzarella cheese
150 mls Sour cream - few sprigs fresh Rosemary
one commercial Pizza Base

<u>To make the Beetroot Jam.</u>
Heat a tablespoon of oil with the mustard seeds until they pop then add
the onions and cook until soft. Add the cloves and saute for a few
minutes. Strain the beetroot and retain the juice. Dice the beetroot and
add to the pan along with the juice, brown sugar and the vinegar.
Simmer until the mixture thickens about thirty minutes. This makes enough
for at least two pizzas and will keep in the fridge in a sterile jar.
Now pre-heat the oven to 250C.
<u>To assemble the Pizza.</u>
Slice and cook the potatoes in the remaining oil until soft. Remove from
the pan and put aside. Fry the remaining onion and diced bacon
in the pan, adding more oil if necessary.
Spread the pizza base with the beetroot jam. Top with the potato slices,
bacon, onions and sprig of rosemary and sprinkle with cheese.
Cook for ten to fifteen minutes until well browned.
Serve with lots of dabs of sour cream.

spicy pumpkin and carrot soup

2 tablespoons Oil - 500gms.peeled & chopped Pumpkin
4 Carrots (chopped) - one Onion diced
500gms. Potatoes (peeled & chopped)
1 Tablespoon Thai Red curry paste - 2 cups Water
270 mls. Coconut Cream - 750 mls. chicken or vegetable stock
12 shelled green King Prawns
chopped fresh Coriander - Juice of a Lime .

Heat the oil in a pan and cook the onions until soft.
Add the curry paste and cook for a further minute.
Stir in the vegetables and cook for two minutes. Add the
water and boil gently until all the vegetables are soft,
adding a little more water if needed.
Liquidise and return the soup to the pan, add the coconut milk
and return to the heat and stir in.
In another saucepan, poach the prawns in salted water until they
are pink through, then drain.
Spoon the soup into individual bowls and top with prawns ,
chopped coriander and a squeeze of lime juice.

savoury crab cups

12 Slices of Sandwich Loaf - 225 gms.Cream Cheese
1/4 Cup of Mayonnaise - 2 tablespoons finely chopped Onion
2 tablespoons Milk - teaspoon Horseradish
teaspoon Dijon Mustard
1/4 teaspoon Salt - 1/4 teaspoon Cayenne Pepper
200gms.Tinned Crab meat or Tuna if preferred - Butter for baking.

Remove the crusts of the bread and butter them on one side.
Press each slice, butter side down into the separate moulds of a
muffin tin, folding the edges to close any gaps.
Bake in the oven at 175C. until just browned.

Mix the rest of the ingredients except the crab or tuna in an
ovenproof bowl and bake at 175C. for 15 minutes.
When cool add the crab or tuna to the mix.

When ready to serve, fill the cases and reheat.

fish
and
shellfish

macadamia white fish

Eight White Fish Fillets - 100mls Sour Cream - one Egg yolk
100mls Seeded Mustard - 50mls Milk
150gms chopped salted Macadamia Nuts
tablespoon Brandy - 6 finely chopped Spring Onions
Cracked Pepper

Mix together the cream, mustard, milk, brandy, egg yolk and
onions in a bowl into which you can dip and coat the fish fillets.
After coating each fillet liberally, roll it in the chopped nuts
and lay out on a well greased baking tray and sprinkle with
cracked pepper.

Place the tray in a preheated oven at 180C and bake for
approximately 25 minutes.

Serve with peppered boiled potatoes and snow peas.

barbecued king prawns

2 Cloves Garlic - 2 tablespoons Crushed Chilli
3 Tablespoons Oil - 50 mls white Wine Vinegar
200mls Coconut Milk - 400mls Water - one cup Sugar
2 tablespoons grated Ginger
800gms Green King Prawns (shelled, tails left on)

Heat the oil in a good sized pan and add the garlic, chilli and ginger, making sure they are all well crushed, and keep them moving for about 30 secs. Now add the vinegar, coconut, milk, water and sugar to the pan and bring to the boil. Allow to stand until cool then lay in the prawns to marinate for at least four hours.

Remove the prawns and place them on the hot barbecue plate. Keep back enough of the liquid to baste them with while they cook until they are nice and pink. Meanwhile reboil the rest of the liquid and simmer until reduced by approximately half. Pour this over the fully cooked prawns in a dish and serve them on a bed of rice.

balmain bugs
in lemon and butter

1 kilo of Balmain Bugs (lobster if not available)
150mls white Wine - 2 Lemons - 150gms Butter
100mls Fish Stock - tablespoon Corn Flour
Clove of Garlic - Black Pepper

Split the bugs down the back in symmetrical halves and brush the
surface of the meat with lemon juice. In a not too big baking dish
melt 75 gms of butter with 50mls of white wine, a pinch of salt, the
juice of half a lemon and a good grinding of black pepper.
Place the bugs, meat side down on the tray and bake in the oven
at 200C. for about 15 minutes.
While they are baking, melt the other 75gms of butter in a saucepan
with 100mls of white wine, the juice of half a lemon, 100 mls of
fish stock, a tablespoon of corn flour and a crushed garlic clove.
Reduce to a nice consistency adding black pepper as you stir.
Pour over the cooked bugs and serve with lemon slices on
a bed of saffron rice.

barramundi fillets
with kiwifruit in bamboo leaves

This recipe is for two fillets but can be adjusted to suit
number of diners.
Two Barramundi Fillets - 1 Pkt. of Bamboo Leaves
Tablespoon Brown Sugar - One Lemon - Teaspoon fresh Ginger
One or Two Kiwifruit (depending on fillet size)
Salt and Black Pepper

Lay out the two fillets and brush well all over with the juice of
the lemon. Sprinkle them both sides with salt and a good
grinding of black pepper.
Peel the kiwifruit and cut into slices. Lay the slices over the main
body of one fillet and sprinkle all over with the brown sugar
and the teaspoon of fresh ginger (grated finely).
Now place the second fillet on top of the first, sandwiching the fruit.
Wrap them carefully in the bamboo leaves and tie with twine.
(If leaves not available, aluminium foil can be used)
Preheat the oven to 150C and bake the fish on a tray for
about 25 minutes.
Can be served in the leaves or unwrapped, garnished with a
little parsley and with boiled new potatoes.

baby octopus
in riverland shiraz

1 Kg.of Baby Octopus - 100 mls. Olive Oil - six sprigs Rosemary
two large fresh Tomatoes - 300 mls. Shiraz
2 medium sized Onions chopped - Salt and Black Pepper
chopped Parsley - 2 cloves Garlic.

Ask your fishmonger to clean and debeak the octopus.
Wash them thoroughly and put aside to drain.
Heat the oil in a saucepan and while very hot toss in the octopus
and sear all surfaces quickly. Reduce the heat a little and add
the onions and crushed garlic and stir until the onions
soften. Chop the tomatoes and add them to the pan together
with two sprigs rosemary, salt to taste, the wine and lots of freshly
ground black pepper. Stir for a few minutes then cover
and simmer gently for one hour.
Decorate with rosemary, serve with a salad and crusty bread.

chilli
blue swimmer crab

4 Blue Swimmer Crabs - 1 Large Onion - 2 Cloves of Garlic
2 Red Chillis - tablespoon Tabasco Sauce - tablespoon Sherry
tablespoon Brown Sugar - Teaspoon chopped fresh Ginger
1/2 cup boiling Water - 100 mls. Olive Oil - 50 gms.Butter

Ask your fish market to clean your crabs and remove the hard
topshell. Wash them thoroughly and cut each crab in halves
and break off the larger claws and crack them before cooking.

In a large heavy pan or wok, heat the oil and fry the finely chopped
onion, garlic,ginger and the chillis, sliced thinly, for 3 or 4 minutes.
Add the sugar, sherry and tabasco sauce as you stir. Now pour in
the boiling water and the crab pieces and simmer with a lid for
eight minutes more, by which time the crabs should be pink.
Now melt the butter and add it, stirring for a further 30 seconds.

Serve immediately with rice and fresh crusty bread.

meat
and
poultry

christmas ham
with pineapple glaze

One cooked Ham on the Bone - 1/4 cup Mustard
Cup dark brown Sugar - 2 cups pineapple juice
6 slices fresh Pineapple - teaspoon Ground Ginger
1/2 cup Port - 20 Cloves.

Peel the skin from the ham and trim the fat to an even thickness.
Score the fat into a diamond pattern, taking care not to cut
down to the meat. Rub the mustard all over the ham and
insert a clove into the intersection of each diamond and
place the ham in a roasting pan.
For the glaze: Heat the pineapple juice, brown sugar and ginger
together and simmer for 5 minutes then pour over the ham.
Cook the ham at 180C. for up to one and a half hours,
depending on the size or until it is nicely browned.
Baste every 15 minutes. Place the pineapple pieces and the port
in the bottom of the pan for the last half hour, continuing to baste.

Turn the ham onto a serving dish and decorate with the pineapple.
Retain the juices from the pan to serve when sliced, thickening with
cornflour if necessary.

meat loaf
with honey and mustard

500 Gms of Premium Minced Beef - 500 Gms of Sausage Mince
One Large Onion - Two Slices of Bread - 2 Tablespoons Honey
3 tablespoons Chopped Parsley - 2 Teaspoons Mustard Powder
A Large Egg - Two Teaspoons Salt - Ground Black Pepper

Finely chop the onion. Dice the slices of bread into pieces
about 4 mm square. Place the beef and the sausage mince
in a large bowl and mix together well. Lightly beat the egg
and add this to the mix together with the bread, onion, salt,
parsley and a liberal grinding of black pepper. Mix all the
ingredients thoroughly. Press the mix into a well greased
loaf tin of approx 24cm length, with the back of a wooden
spoon. Cover with foil, place in the preheated oven at
180 C and cook for about one hour.
Now blend the mustard powder with enough water to make
a paste in a cup and add the Honey.
When the cooking time is up, drain off excess liquid, make
a series of 1cm deep cuts in the top and spread the mix
into them with a knife.
Cook for a further 20 minutes without the foil.

rack of lamb
with mango sauce

4 Lamb racks (3 or 4 cutlets each) - Salt to taste - Black Pepper
Olive oil - 5 Mangoes - 1 Lime - Teaspoon Fresh Grated Ginger
1/4 cup of Port - 2 Tablespoons Brown Sugar - 1/4 cup Sour Cream
1 Tablespoon of Ketjap Manis (indonesian soy sauce)

Place the racks in a baking dish, brush with olive oil and season
with salt and freshly ground black pepper. Now put them in a
preheated oven at 180C and bake for 15 minutes.
To make the sauce, peel the mangoes and cut the flesh into
reasonably large slices. Into a food processor place the flesh of
two mangoes, the juice of the lime, the fresh ginger, port,
sour cream, Ketjap Manis, salt to taste and the sugar.
Liquidise until creamy. Transfer to a pan and simmer until required.

Remove the racks temporarily and baste them with some of the
sauce and add the remaining mango slices to the dish.
Continue to bake, basting occasionally, for a further 15 minutes.
The rest of the sauce should be kept for use at the time of serving
with garlic roasted or boiled potatoes.

aussie meat pies

550 gms Flour - 300 gms of cold Butter - teaspoon of Salt
250 mls of Iced Water - Olive Oil - Bouquet Garni
900 gms of Rump Steak diced and rolled in flour - one Onion
1 cup of Beef Stock - 1 Egg Yolk -   ground Black Pepper

Sift 500 Gms. flour and the salt into a bowl and rub in100Gms.
butter. Mix to a dough using the cold water and a knife. Roll
out onto a floured surface. Grate a further third of the butter
over the centre half of the dough, fold in the flaps and roll out well.
Repeat with the last third then fold up and refrigerate while
preparing the meat. Dice the steak and place in a bag with 50 Gms.
flour with salt and pepperand shake until coated. Put a little olive oil
into a saucepan over medium heat and cook the onion for a few
minutes then add the steak and brown it. Add the stock, bouquet
garni and a liberal grinding of fresh black pepper and simmer until
the beef is tender. Set aside to cool after removing the bouquet.
Now bring out the pastry and roll out
thinly again. Cut six 17cm.circles and six 12.5cm circles. Press the
larger ones into the bottom of six 11cm. pie tins, fill with the meat,
brush the edges of the pastry with the beaten egg yolk, add the tops
and press the edges down with a fork.
Paint the tops with a little more egg yolk and cut 2 or 3 slits for
the meat to breathe. Bake in a hot oven until the pastry has browned
(approx. 20 Minutes).

chicken and apricot coconut curry

500 gms.Chicken Breast - two tablespoons Oil
425 gm.tin of Apricots in natural Juice
One teaspoon minced Garlic - one teaspoon ground Coriander
4 or 5 Fenugreek seeds - one teaspoon minced Garlic
One tablespoon Madras Curry Paste - 120 mls. Coconut Cream
One tablespoon minced Ginger - one Onion chopped
One cup Basmati Rice - Poppadums (cooked)

Gently saute the chopped onion in the oil with the garlic
and ginger for five minutes. Add the curry paste, stir and
simmer another few minutes. Add the coriander,
fenugreek and the chicken pieces and cook gently for ten
minutes, stirring now and then until the chicken is cooked evenly.
Now add one cup of apricot juice from the tin with 8-10 apricot
halves and the coconut cream. Simmer until the sauce thickens.
Serve on a bed of boiled rice, sprinkle with dessicated coconut
and add the poppadums.

surf and turf
with sherry sauce

2 Scotch Fillets - 6 large King Prawns - tablespoon Oil
teaspoon chopped Garlic - 30 gms.Butter - 150 mls.Cream
tablespoon of chopped Onion - 2 Egg Yolks
5 tablespoons of Sherry - teaspoon of Mustard

To make the sauce. Melt the butter and soften the onions. Add the
sherry and simmer for five minutes. Mix the egg yolks with
the cream and stir into pan. Add one teaspoon of mustard and
season. Simmer over a gentle heat for a further five minutes,
stirring until the sauce thickens. Do not allow the sauce to boil.
Add the oil to a solid bottomed pan and when hot throw in the
prawns and fry until pink through. Now remove the prawns
and put aside to keep hot and add the steaks to the pan with the
garlic. Sear them both sides about one minute each on high
then reduce the heat a little and continue cooking each side to taste.

Serve the steak and prawns together with the sherry sauce and
for example, saute potatoes. Serves two.

vegetables
and
salads

ocean trout salad

6 boiled New Potatoes (quartered) - one Lime
100 Gms. halved salted Macadamia Nuts
2 vine ripened Tomatoes (quartered) - 5 or 6 Lettuce leaves
1 green Capsicum (cored and chopped) - 3 spring Onions (chopped)
2 hardboiled Eggs (quartered) - Salt and Black Pepper
1 dozen Black Olives - 500 Gms. poached Ocean Trout
Olive Oil and Balsamic vinegar for dressing

On a platter make a bed of the lettuce leaves.
Place the eggs on top. In a bowl, toss the potatoes, nuts,
tomatoes, capsicum, onions, and olives together and
turn out onto the lettuce.
Dress pieces of ocean trout on the top and sprinkle the
whole dish with balsamic vinegar and olive oil. Season with
the salt and pepper and lime juice.
Serve with fresh bread.

chilli pumpkin
with macadamia butter

800 gms. Pumpkin - A large brown Onion
2 Tablespoons of Macadamia Oil
2 teaspoons of hot Chilli Paste - 125 gms. Macadamia Butter

Peel the pumpkin, remove the seeds and chop into chunks.
Add the pumpkin to a pan of salted boiling water and cook
until soft to a fork.
Drain off the water and mash the pumpkin then set it aside.

Heat the oil in a solid pan and add the finely chopped onion and
the chilli paste. Cook gently until they soften. Now blend this
with the previously mashed pumpkin and stir in the
macadamia butter (peanut if not available) .
Serve hot garnished with chopped chives.

spicy potato
with kumerah and carrot

---

500 gms. Potatoes - 400 gms Kumerah - 4 Carrots
5 tablespoons Oil - 1/2 teaspoon Brown Mustard Seeds
2 Onions chopped - 3 dried red Chillis - 2 fresh green Chillies
teaspoon ground Turmeric - Salt and Black Pepper
chopped Coriander for Garnish.

Peel and dice the potatoes and kumerah and skin and slice
the carrots, put them together in a saucepan of boiling salted water
and cook almost through but not until soft. Drain and set aside.
In an electric frypan or large pan, heat the oil with the mustard
seeds until tthey pop then add the onions and chillis and
continue stirring until the onions brown. Put in the turmeric
and all the part cooked vegetables and turn them occasionally
for about ten minutes at which time they should be hot and
ready to serve garnished with the chopped coriander.

lobster and rockmelon salad
with coconut and mint

---

500 gms. diced Rockmelon - 500 gms. Lobster meat.
3 sticks of Celery chopped - small Lettuce
tablespoon Honey - 250 mls. Sour Cream - 2 tablespoons
tablespoon chopped Mint - 2 tablespoons Mint Sauce
3 tablespoons freshly grated Coconut.

Mix together the honey, mint, sour cream and the
mint sauce in a large bowl.
In another bowl, combine the lobster meat, melon and the
celery. Add to the cream mixture and combine gently.
Arrange the mixture on a serving plate on a bed of the
lettuce leaves and sprinkle with the freshly grated coconut.

pasta and rice

tagliatelli
with western australian scampi

8 green Western Australian Scampi - 500 gms.Tagliatelli
100 gms.Butter - 2 cloves of Garlic crushed - Salt & Pepper
8 Asparagus spears - 200 mls.cream - pinch of Saffron
tablespoon chopped Chives - tablespoon of Lemon Juice
100 mls. Sarantos Chardonnay

In a large pan boil 2 1/2 litres of water with a
tablespoon of salt . Add the tagliatelli and simmer for about
10 minutes or until tender (al dente), then drain.
At the same time in a solid bottomed pan, melt the butter
and add garlic and the white wine. Simmer for five minutes.
Split the scampi down the back in symmetrical halves and clean
them. Brush the surface of the meat with lemon juice and saute in
the wine mixture until pink through. Remove from the pan and
keep them warm. Add the cream and saffron to the pan.
Simmer until the sauce thickens. Cut the asparagus into small
pieces, add to the sauce and simmer for another two minutes.
Drain the pasta and while still very hot, add the sauce and the
chopped chives. Season to taste, serve into separate bowls,
and top with the scampi.

bacon and pumpkin risotto

2 cups Arborio Rice - 1 Onion chopped
350 gms.Pumpkin peeled, cubed and cooked until just soft
One cup of cooked Green Peas - 30 gms. Butter
Salt & Pepper to taste
clove of Garlic pressed - half teaspoon ground Coriander
Litre hot Chicken or Vegetable stock - Half cup of white Wine
half Cup of Orange Juice - half teaspoon ground Coriander
4 Rashers Bacon grilled & diced - fresh Coriander for garnish

Melt the butter and soften the onion. Add the garlic and the
ground coriander and cook for two minutes. Add the rice and stir
until coated in the butter. Now add the wine and the juice and
continually stir the rice while adding the stock a cupfull at a time.
When the rice is cooked and the liquid absorbed, add the peas,
pumpkin and bacon and continue to stir until warmed through. Serve
topped with the chopped coriander.

Our family prefers this risotto, Milanese Style, creamy but with the
grains cooked completely through.

almond pesto penne
with sundried tomatoes
and tasmanian feta

500 gms. Penne - 2 cups Basil Leaves - 4 tablespoons Olive Oil
4 tablespoons crushed Almonds - 2 peeled cloves of Garlic
175 gm. chopped Sundried Tomatoes - 200 mls.Cream
200 gms.Tasmanian Feta Cheese - Salt and Pepper

Heat a tablespoon of the oil in a solid frying pan and add the well
crushed garlic and the nuts and fry until golden, then set aside.
Remove the stems from the basil, discard them and wash the
leaves well. At this stage begin to cook the penne in a saucepan of
salted boilingwater for about 12 minutes or until 'Al Dente'.
While this is cooking, slowly add the garlic, nuts, basil, the rest of
the oil and the cream to your blender until smooth.
When the pasta is ready, drain and while still piping hot, turn the
blended mixture through it.

Dress the top of each serving with the feta in 1cm. cubes,
sundried tomatoes and lots of black pepper.

weights and measures

temperature

	C	F
cool	100	200
moderate	180	350
mod.hot	190	375
hot	220	425
v.hot	240	475

weights

15gms.	1/2 oz.
30gms.	1 oz.
60gms	2 ozs.
125gms	4 ozs.
250gms	8 ozs.
375gms.	12 ozs.
500gms.	1 lb.
1kg.	2 lbs.

measurements

5mm	1/4 inch
1cm.	1/2 inch
5cm.	2 inches
12cm.	5 inches
18cm.	7 inches
23cm.	9 inches
30cm.	12 inches

liquid

5mls	1/6 fl.oz.	teaspoon
20mls.	2/3 fl.oz.	tablespoon
60mls.	2 fl.ozs.	1/4 cup
125mls.	4 fl.ozs.	1/2 cup
250mls.	8 fl.ozs.	1 cup
500mls	16 fl.ozs.	2 cups
1 litre	1 3/4 pts	4 cups

bread cakes and biscuits

anzac biscuits

1 cup of Flour - 1 cup of Rolled Oats
3/4 cup of Sugar - 3/4 cup of Desiccated coconut
1 teaspoon of Bicarbonate of Soda
2 tablespoons of boiling Water
2 tablespoons of Golden Syrup
100 gms of Butter.

Sift the flour and bi-carbonate of soda into a bowl and
add the oats, coconut and sugar.
Into a saucepan containing the boiling water add the
butter and the golden syrup and stir well over the heat.
Pour this into the dry ingredients and mix well.
Dish out the mix in dessertspoonfuls, roll into a ball and
slightly flatten. Place on a lightly greased baking tray with
about 3cms. between each.
Bake in the middle of your oven pre-heated to 150 C. for
approximately 20 minutes.
Makes 15 - 18 biscuits.

damper
with cocky's joy

3 cups of Flour
1 1/2 teaspoons Salt
2 teaspoons Bicarbonate of Soda
2 tablespoons Butter
2 tablespoons Milk
Water.

Sift the flour into a bowl with the salt and the bicarbonate of soda. Make a well in the centre and add the milk and the previously melted butter. Begin mixing, adding water as you go to make a kneadable dough. Turn out onto a floured surface and knead for a minute or so. Roll the dough into a ball and then flatten to about eight centimetres high.
The damper is then traditionally cooked in the bush by burying it in the ashes of the fire until it sounds hollow when tapped. However it can be placed on a tray in your oven for approx. 20 minutes at pre-heated 190 C. Serve hot with butter, golden syrup (cocky's joy) or honey.

lamingtons

240gms. Plain Flour - 100gms. Butter - 160gms. Caster Sugar
2 large eggs - 2 teaspoons Baking Powder
125mls. Milk - 1 1/4 Teaspoons Vanilla Essence - 1/4 teaspoon Salt
3 cups Dessicated Coconut - 3 cups Icing Sugar - Strawberry Jam
1/2 cup Cocoa Powder - 1/4 cup boiling Water - 3/4 cup of cream

Combine the butter and sugar in your electric mixer bowl
until light and creamy then add a teaspoon of vanilla and the
beaten eggs. Sift the flour, baking powder and salt
together and add little by little to the mix, aerating with
the milk. Pour the mix into a shallow pre-greased tin approx
25cm square. Bake in a preheated oven for about 30-40
minutes at 180C. Turn the cake out and when it is cold,
trim it and cut it in half horizontally. Whip the cream and
spread the jam and cream evenly between the two layers.
Now sift the icing sugar into a bowl and add the cocoa, the
rest of the vanilla and the boiling water. Stand the bowl in a
saucepan of simmering water and stir until smooth and
liquid. Cut the cake into 5cm squares, coat them in the
mix and roll each one in the coconut.

gem scones

60gms.of Butter - 85 gms.of Caster Sugar
225 gms.of self raising Flour
85 mls. of Milk (approx)
1 Egg - Vanilla Essence - Pinch of Salt

A "Gem Iron" is a set of twelve cast iron hemisphere joined together. As the batter rises to a dome a round cake results. If you do not have such a thing then a muffin tin is the next best item.

Place the gem iron in the oven to pre-heat. First cream together the butter, sugar, and vanilla. Add the lightly beaten egg and whisk the mixture well. Sift together the flour and the salt and fold them into the mixture slowly, using the milk intermittently to make a mixture the consistency of cake batter. Half fill each segment of the gem iron and return to the hot oven quickly. Bake for about 12-15 minutes .
Turn out to cool a little.
They are best served still warm with butter in the middle.
This mix should make two trays.

ingredient alternatives

Apricots--Peach halves
Arborio Rice--Long grain rice
Balmain Bugs--Lobstertails or Crayfish
Bamboo Leaves--Paperbark or Aluminium foil
Barramundi--any thick fleshed white Fish
Blue Swimmer Crabs--Any type of fresh Crab
Bouquet Garni--Small Parcel of Herbs
Crabmeat--Tinned Tuna
Cocky's Joy--Golden Syrup or Treacle
Plain Flour--All purpose Flour
Ketjap Manis--Soy Sauce and Sugar
King Prawns--Large Shrimp
Kiwifruit--Any Tropical Fruit
Kumerah--Sweet Potato or Yams
Macadamia Butter--Peanut Butter
Macadamia Nuts--Peanuts or Cashews
Macadamia Oil--Peanut or Vegetable Oil
Mango--Tinned mango or Peaches
Mascarpone--Thick cream
Ocean Trout--Salmon
Passionfruit--Tinned Passionfruit Pulp
Rockmelon--Any firm Melon
Scampi--Deepsea Lobster or Crayfish
Shiraz--Any full bodied red Wine
Sundried Tomatoes--Oven Dried or Preserved
Tasmanian Feta--Greek or Marinated Feta

desserts

passionfruit custard ice cream

500 mls.of Milk - 200gms. Sugar
tablespoon of Cornflour - 8 Egg Yolks lightly beaten
1/4 teaspoon of Salt - 600mls. Cream
tablespoon of Vanilla Essence - 5 Passionfruit

Scald 375mls. of milk in a saucepan. Add 100gms. of
sugar and stir until dissolved. In another bowl mix the dry
cornflour with the rest of the sugar. Add the other 125mls. of cold
milk and mix well. Blend this slowly with the hot milk
mixture while beating. Simmer gently, stirring all the while until
the mixture thickens. Beat the egg yolks and and add to the
hot mix. Continue beating so that the eggs do not scramble. Cook
for two minutes. When the mix is cool, add the salt, cream,
vanilla and the pulp of three passionfruits. Freeze the mix for
two hours then rebeat and freeze again.

Serve topped with fresh Passionfruit pulp.

pavlova

6 Egg Whites - 350 gms. Caster Sugar
teaspoon Salt - 600 mls Cream
3 Kiwifruit - 250 gms.Cream Cheese - 3 Bananas sliced
3 Passionfruit - juice & finely grated rind of one Lemon.
2 tablespoons sugar extra for cream mix.

Place the egg whites and salt in a bowl and whisk until they
will stand in peaks. Add 1/4 of the sugar slowly, beating
continuously until it is completely dissolved. Fold in the remaining
sugar with a metal spoon. Now lay a sheet of foil onto a
baking tray and spread the mix carefully onto it to form a disk
approximately 20 cm. Diameter.
Place in a preheated oven at 120 C for about 2 to 3 hours.
Switch off the oven and leave the meringue in the oven until
cool. Beat the cheese with one dessertspoon of lemon juice, grated
rind, and the extra sugar. Whip the cream and add half to the
cheese with the bananas. Spoon the cheese mixture
onto the meringue and top the remaining cream. Decorate with the
passionfruit pulp and the peeled and sliced kiwifruit.

summerfruits
with mascarpone

800 gms. available summer fruits such as..
Blueberries - Strawberries - Raspberries - Peaches
Melon - Nectarines - two tablespoons Caster Sugar
100 mls. Botrytis Dessert Wine - 50 mls. Water

---

250 Gms. Mascarpone Cheese - tablespoon Caster Sugar
two tablespoons Botrytis Dessert Wine

Simmer the water with 100 mls. wine and 2 tablespoons of
caster sugar until dissolved. Add the fruit, cover and simmer
for one minute only then set aside to cool in the syrup.

Add to the cheese, one tablespoon of caster sugar and two
tablespoons of the wine and mix until well blended.
Spoon the cooled fruit into parfait glasses with very little syrup and
top with the mascarpone.

tamarillos
with praline cream

8 Tamarillos - 2 cups Sugar - 2 Cups Water - 1 Vanilla Bean
4 Egg Yolks - 1 tablespoon Caster Sugar - tablespoon Cornflour
600 Mls. Cream - Vanilla essence - 100 Gms Vienna Almonds.

Peel the tamarillos, taking care not to break into the flesh.
In a medium sized pot, bring the water to the boil and add
the sugar and the vanilla bean and stir until the sugar dissolves.
Put the tamarillos into the liquid, bring back to the simmer
and continue until they are tender then allow them to cool
in the syrup.

To make the cream mixture, whisk the egg yolks, caster sugar and
cornflour in a bowl until they thicken. In a seperate pan, bring the
cream just to boiling point, then add it to the mixture stirring
constantly. Return all this to the pan and continue stirring over
gentle heat until it will thickly coat the back of a spoon. Pour into
individual ramekins and chill. Serve the tamarillos on a plate with
their syrup, with a ramekin of cream mixture on the side, over which
you should sprinkle the toffeed almonds after turning them to praline
in your blender.

index